COUNTING WITH HEARTS

WRITTEN BY: MELISSA L. BRYANT

I DEDICATE THIS BOOK TO MY GRANDCHILDREN, NIECES, NEPHEWS AND CHILDREN AROUND THE WORLD. I HOPE YOU ENJOY LEARNING HOW TO COUNT WITH HEARTS. LEARNING IS FUN.

1

I SEE ONE HEART. HOW MANY DO YOU SEE?

I SEE TWO HEARTS. HOW MANY DO YOU SEE?

I SEE THREE HEARTS. HOW MANY DO YOU SEE?

I SEE FOUR HEARTS. HOW MANY DO YOU SEE?

I SEE FIVE HEARTS. HOW MANY DO YOU SEE?

I SEE SIX HEARTS. HOW MANY DO YOU SEE?

I SEE SEVEN HEARTS. HOW MANY DO YOU SEE?

I SEE EIGHT HEARTS. HOW MANY DO YOU SEE?

I SEE NINE HEARTS. HOW MANY DO YOU SEE?

I SEE TEN HEARTS. HOW MANY DO YOU SEE?

I SEE ELEVEN HEARTS. HOW MANY DO YOU SEE?

I SEE TWELVE HEARTS. HOW MANY DO YOU SEE?

I SEE THIRTEEN HEARTS. HOW MANY DO YOU SEE?

I SEE FOURTEEN HEARTS. HOW MANY DO YOU SEE?

I SEE FIFTHTEEN HEARTS. HOW MANY DO YOU SEE?

I SEE SIXTEEN HEARTS. HOW MANY DO YOU SEE?

I SEE SEVENTEEN HEARTS. HOW MANY DO YOU SEE?

I SEE EIGHTEEN HEARTS. HOW MANY DO YOU SEE?

I SEE NINETEEN HEARTS. HOW MANY DO YOU SEE?

I SEE TWENTY HEARTS. HOW MANY DO YOU SEE?

HOW MANY HEARTS DO YOU SEE?